INTO
Wild Tasmania

BLACKBIRCH PRESS

An imprint of Thomson Gale, a part of The Thomson Corporation

THOMSON

™

GALE

Detroit • New York • San Francisco • San Diego • New Haven, Conn. • Waterville, Maine • London • Munich

THOMSON

—★—

GALE

LIBRARY OF CONGRESS CATALOGING-IN-PUBLICATION DATA

Into wild Tasmania / Marla Ryan, book editor.
 p. cm. — (The Jeff Corwin experience)
 Includes bibliographical references and index.
 ISBN 1-4103-0247-4 (alk. paper) — ISBN 1-4103-0248-2 (pbk. : alk. paper)
 1. Tanzania—Description and travel—Juvenile literature. 2. Zoology—Tanzania—Juvenile literature. 3. Natural history—Tanzania—Juvenile literature. 4. Wilderness areas—Tanzania—Juvenile literature. 5. Corwin, Jeff—Travel—Tanzania—Juvenile literature. I. Ryan, Marla Felkins. II. Corwin, Jeff. III. Series.

 DT440.5.I583 2004
 590'.9678—dc22   2004004487

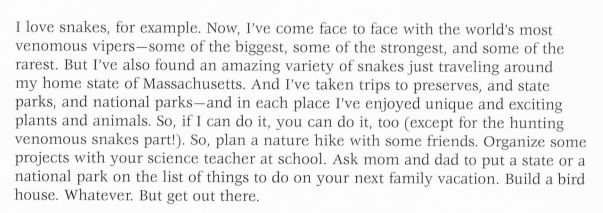

Ever since I was a kid, I dreamed about traveling around the world, visiting exotic places, and seeing all kinds of incredible animals. And now, guess what? That's exactly what I get to do!

Yes, I am incredibly lucky. But, you don't have to have your own television show on Animal Planet to go off and explore the natural world around you. I mean, I travel to Madagascar and the Amazon and all kinds of really cool places—but I don't need to go that far to see amazing wildlife up close. In fact, I can find thousands of incredible critters right here, in my own backyard—or in my neighbor's yard (he does get kind of upset when he finds me crawling around in the bushes, though). The point is, no matter where you are, there's fantastic stuff to see in nature. All you have to do is look.

I love snakes, for example. Now, I've come face to face with the world's most venomous vipers—some of the biggest, some of the strongest, and some of the rarest. But I've also found an amazing variety of snakes just traveling around my home state of Massachusetts. And I've taken trips to preserves, and state parks, and national parks—and in each place I've enjoyed unique and exciting plants and animals. So, if I can do it, you can do it, too (except for the hunting venomous snakes part!). So, plan a nature hike with some friends. Organize some projects with your science teacher at school. Ask mom and dad to put a state or a national park on the list of things to do on your next family vacation. Build a bird house. Whatever. But get out there.

As you read through these pages and look at the photos, you'll probably see how jazzed I get when I come face to face with beautiful animals. That's good. I want you to feel that excitement. And I want you to remember that—even if you don't have your own TV show—you can still experience the awesome beauty of nature almost anywhere you go—any day of the week. I only hope that I can help bring that awesome power and beauty a little closer to you. Enjoy!

Best Wishes!

Jeff

INTO
Wild Tasmania

NORTH
AMERICA

Atlantic
Ocean

Pacific
Ocean

SOUTH
AMERICA

EUROPE

AFRICA

ASIA

Indian
Ocean

Pacific
Ocean

AUSTRALIA

It's serene, it's beautiful, and it's dangerous. It has poisonous snakes and mammals that lay eggs. And it has the devil—the Tasmanian devil, that is. Join me as we explore a land filled with wildlife, much of it found nowhere else.

I'm Jeff Corwin.
Welcome to Tasmania.

Tasmania

Honeycomb Caves

Hobart

Tasman Peninsula

Ready to start our adventure?

Australia is "the land down under," and Tasmania is the land down under the land down under. Our expedition will take us down the spine of Tasmania from north to south, and all sorts of creatures are on our list to find here. But we're going to start by going deeper under the down under—into Honeycomb Cave, to find a spider that lives nowhere but here. . .

Let's venture into Honeycomb Cave.

The Tasmanian cave spider is an ancient creature.

This is a Tasmanian cave spider, a great introduction into the world of Tasmanian wildlife. It's a beautiful invertebrate. Although it's not dangerous, it can bite, so I'm being careful. I can just ease it up on my hands. It's an ancient creature. These spiders have been around practically unchanged for 200 million years. They're very primitive in their design. And for scientists, they serve as a bridge between the spiders of prehistoric times and those of modern times.

If you want to find this spider's closest relatives, you have go all the way to South America, to Chile. Think about that: Why is the nearest cousin of this spider found in Chile? Well, the ancestors of both spiders lived hundreds of millions of years ago, when South

America and Australia were joined to a super-continent called Gondwanaland. When Gondwanaland broke apart, two populations of spiders were separated, and they evolved into two species. One lives here in Tasmania, and the other lives in Chile.

This spider hasn't changed in millions of years.

Honeycomb Cave is great, but there's more wonderful stuff to be discovered above. From this system of caves, we're going to head south and west through Cradle Mountain National Park. Then we'll move back to the east to an area called Trowunna. From there we'll head to Hobart, the capital city. Then, a little farther south, we'll come face-to-face with one of the fiercest creatures on the planet.

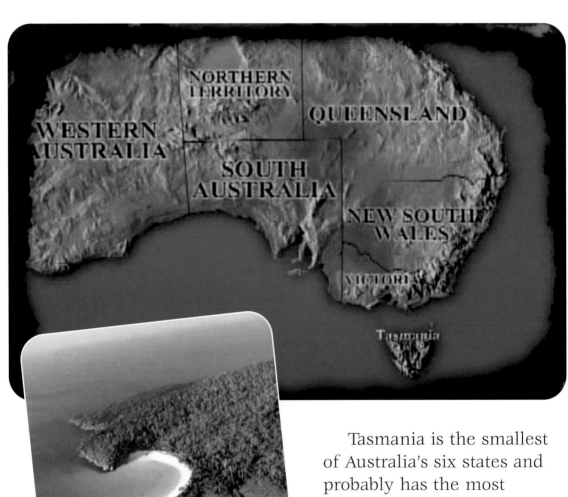

Tasmania's landscape is made up of beautiful coastlines...

Tasmania is the smallest of Australia's six states and probably has the most unique character. It is completely isolated from the rest of the country, so there are animals here that are now extinct on the mainland.

lush farmland...

raging rivers...

oceanfront cities...

The landscape of Tasmania is diverse and dramatic. It has everything from farmland to oceanfront cities, from rugged mountain peaks to world-class vineyards. It is a paradise for adventurists like myself.

expansive vineyards...

colorful caves...

and rugged mountains.

Got to get that snake.

But before we leave this cave system, there's a snake out there just waiting for me. I can see shiny scales, a dark body, a tail . . . .

This guy gave me a run for my money, but I got him and he's beautiful. He's a lowland copperhead, an adult. And like all the snakes in Tasmania he's venomous.

These creatures are very well adapted to deal with changes in temperature. And that's important if you live in Tasmania, especially in the mountains, because the temperature can drop suddenly. One minute it's hot, and then night comes and, even in summertime, temperatures drop down in the high forties.

This is a lowland copperhead.

The way this snake's young are born helps it succeed in these cold temperatures. Most snakes are oviparous. That is, they lay eggs. But the lowland copperhead is ovoviviparous. Instead of laying eggs, the mother retains her young in her body inside an egglike membrane. That keeps them warm as the young develop. When the membrane ruptures, she gives birth to live young.

Look at the eyes—see how they're kind of foggy? My guess is that this snake is not far from shedding its skin. These animals eat all sorts of things—small rodents, small marsupials, skinks. Interestingly, they can also be cannibalistic. Look at the head. That cinnamon color is what gave rise to the name copperhead. It's a gorgeous snake. I'll gently place it back in the place where we found it, and continue our journey into the mountains of Tasmania.

He's beautiful, venomous, and not too happy right now.

That's Cradle Mountain. Breathtaking!

Cradle Mt. Nat'l Park

We're on our way to quoll country.

Next stop on our southward journey is Cradle Mountain National Park. As in much of Tasmania, the scenery here is breathtaking. We're here with Diane Moyle, a researcher from the University of Tasmania. She's an expert on eastern quolls, catlike marsupials that are unique to this island.

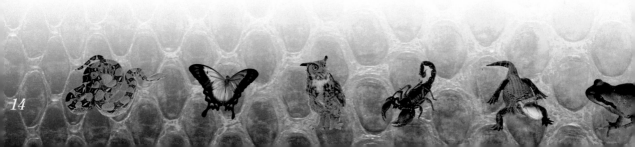

Di is studying a population of quolls on a site that covers about fourteen hectares here. It's prime quoll country because there's limestone under the soil. As the limestone breaks down and washes away, it leaves sinkholes that quolls can use as burrows.

Diane is a quoll expert.

Based on that, and lots of quoll scat, Di is pretty sure there's a large breeding population of quolls here. She has set some traps, and we check them.

Check this out. We've got a quoll, and a fairly unusual one. It's a subtype that appears in about one of every fourteen quolls. This is

A quoll is a catlike marsupial.

I'll just put this quoll down before she bites me.

a female, and she looks like she wants to bite. Di says she won't, but just to be on the safe side I'll pop her in this bag. She'll calm down in a second.

Next we find a young male, a black one. These animals are meat eaters, hunting and scavenging for beetles, grubs, and even mice and larger animals. At one time they were very common on mainland Australia. But they were driven to extinction there, mostly because of the impact of animals such as foxes, cats, and dogs that were introduced by Europeans. Dogs killed quolls, and feral cats and foxes competed with quolls for food. The quolls were unable to adapt to the challenge.

The last place you can find quolls is in Tasmania. There are lots of them here because the numbers of feral cats and foxes are extremely low. In the past foxes were released here, but Tasmanian

devils kept their numbers in check. The tassie devils would raid fox dens and eat the fox pups.

There is concern now that the population of foxes will increase. If foxes get a grip in Tasmania, you can kiss the quoll good-bye—and what a tragedy that would be.

We'll let this animal go and continue on our way.

These marsupials are found only in Tasmania.

Trowunna wildlife sanctuary is home to kangaroos...

wombats...

even echidnas!

We've left Cradle Mountain National Park. We're now in the outskirts of Mole Creek Village, at the Trowunna wildlife sanctuary. This is a place where orphaned and captive-bred animals can live in a protected environment. Home to thirty-five different species, it is a refuge for Tasmanian creatures both big and small.

Look at this. It's a baby wombat, just four months old and still very fragile. It's still growing its fur, and it looks like a rodent of some sort. But it's not a rodent; it's a marsupial. And like other marsupials, baby wombats spend their first months of life in the mother's pouch, nursing. This little one will need to be in the pouch for two or three months more.

Don't bite too hard, little one.

Adult wombats are another story.

Each year hundreds of animals just like this are orphaned. Lucky ones are hand raised at Trowunna and eventually released into the wild. But Trowunna also has a large population of wild wombats.

Adult wombats can be somewhat territorial. And if they feel threatened, they can be tricky in their behavior. If you want to get close, the secret is to move very slowly and quietly—just creep in.

These creatures are master diggers.

The two things that wombats do best are digging and eating. Wombats are masters at excavating dens into the earth. Their tunnels are often wide enough for a small man to crawl through. And they eat constantly. They're grazers.

Wombats are found throughout Australia. Here in Tasmania, they have few natural enemies—except for the tassie devil, which will attack and eat just about anything that moves. But wombats here have to deal with more environmental extremes, especially up here in the mountains. In winter the ground here is covered with snow. The wombat is protected in its underground tunnels, but even in winter it must come out and eat.

Wombats enjoy easy living all over Australia.

Except in winter, when snow makes it harder to find food.

There's so much more to see here in Trowunna. Just by hiking a bit, we've crossed over into a completely different habitat, one of the coolest forests I've ever moved through. This is an old growth mountain moist forest. Every branch is dripping with moss and lichens.

Moss and lichens blanket this mountain forest.

And check this out. Bouncing on the mattress of spongy moss at my feet is a Tasmanian pademelon. Like kangaroos and wallabies, these animals belong to a group called macropods, from Greek words that mean "large footed." They have big hind legs and hop around like this fellow—*boing, boing, boing.*

There's a pademelon.

The pademelon is one of the cutest macropods you'll ever see. It is the third smallest of the macropods in Tasmania, which include potoroos and bettongs as well as kangaroos and wallabies. It stands about sixteen inches tall and is an excellent hopper. It forages on the forest floor and even goes up into low branches to find moss, seeds, shoots, nuts, and fruits.

What a cute macropod!

And there's her little joey.

We've spotted a mother pademelon with her baby, called a joey, at her side. Pademelons are pretty rare. This species is found only in Tasmania, but in this park they're quite common.

One trait shared by many of the animals here, especially the marsupials, is a fairly short life span. Pademelons live only seven or eight years in the wild; kangaroos and koalas, about ten. They're born, have lots of offspring, and die. If you're a marsupial in these parts, I guess you just live fast and then die young.

Before we leave Trowunna, there are a couple of other creatures I'd like you to meet.

Look at that! That Eastern gray kangaroo has a joey, too.

Those feet are made for jumping.

These are Eastern gray kangaroos, a female and her little joey. Eastern gray kangaroos are the largest marsupials in Tasmania. A male can weigh up to 130 pounds. And if you look down at their feet, you'll understand what macropod means—they really have big feet. These animals can jump high enough to clear a seven-foot fence. On the mainland, when they're being chased by a predator such as a dingo, they'll bound along, zigzagging out of the predators path of attack.

A joey like this is the size of a pea when it's born. It spends the first eleven months of its life inside its mother's pouch. Then, for another seven months, it's outside the pouch but close to mom, partaking of milk.

This joey looks like he wants out, but he has to stay in his mother's pouch until he's eleven months old.

These two are bobbing their ears, as if they were trying to get rid of flies. But there aren't any flies, so the ear bobbing may be a form of communication. It could be a sign of reassurance between mother and joey—sort of, "I'm okay, you're okay."

See how they bob their ears? That's how they talk.

Face-to-face with Eastern gray kangaroos—how's this for an experience?

How cool is it to be this close to kangaroos?

We're face-to-face.

Wow! Now this is something very exciting to see. It's like coming face-to-face with a living fossil. This animal is an echidna, one of an ancient group of mammals.

It's kind of tricky to pick up an echidna because this animal has a pretty good defense. It pulls itself into the earth, burying its face

You can tell she's in defense mode with all those quills sticking out.

So I'll be careful picking her up.

and limbs, and then it exposes an arsenal of quills. This creature's in total defense mode, so I have to dig it out to give you a closer look. There are so many amazing things about echidnas.

Echidnas are specialists when it comes to their diet. Mostly, they eat ants. In a given feeding session, an echidna will eat hundreds and hundreds of ants. It closes its eyes so the ants can't bite its eyes. It sticks that beaklike snout into the ant nest. Then it uses its seven-inch-long

They close their eyes when feeding.

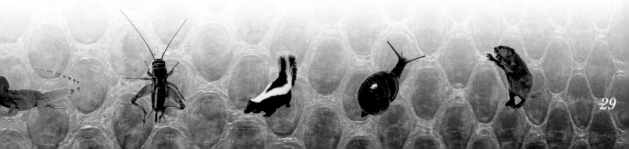

Its seven-inch tongue is perfect for sucking up hose ants.

And its paws are great for digging.

sticky tongue to suck hose ants into its mouth, grinding them up into a delicious ant paste.

Check out the paws. The echidna uses its paws to excavate ant nests, and they're like front-end loaders. They have sharp claws that dig very quickly.

The echidna is a mammal, but what's most amazing about this creature is that it is a mammal that lays eggs. There are two mammals on our planet that lay eggs—the echidna and the platypus—and both are found here in Tasmania.

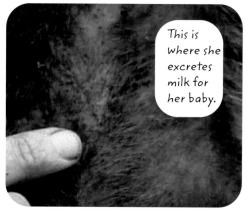

This is where she excretes milk for her baby.

A female echidna lays an egg an average of ten days or so after mating. She will incubate the egg in a pouchlike structure on her body. After twenty days or so the baby hatches. It stays in the pouch for a couple of months. Instead of a nipple, the echidna excretes milk at a region on the skin, through little pores. The baby laps milk from the surface of its mother's skin.

These animals are unusual in another way. They have an exception-ally long life span. They aren't able to reproduce until they're at least five or six years in age, perhaps even later. But they can live fifty years or more.

An echidna, an egg-laying mammal. You can't tell me this doesn't blow your mind.

You are one cool egg-laying mammal!

Eileen studies the duckbill platypus.

We've reached the capital of Tasmania, the very historic and beautiful city of Hobart, to meet up with a friend of mine, Eileen Wronski. She's a biologist and a veterinarian, and she's doing some graduate work with the University of Tasmania. Her study involves an amazing creature—a creature that you have to see if you come to Tasmania. It's the duckbill platypus.

She has set up these traps along a creek.

It's hard to believe, but just twenty minutes from downtown Hobart is some prime platypus habitat. Eileen is doing research on how these animals react to disease, and she has set up a couple of traps along a creek in this area. The traps are almost like lobster traps. They have a system of nets, and once the creature works his way into it he can't get out.

Let's get this guy out.

There's something in this trap, and it's definitely not a lobster. It's a platypus, and a good-size one. Let's get him out and have a look.

Along with his webbed feet, the platypus's broad, flat tail provides locomotion when he's swimming and diving. Check out the spurs on his back feet. The spurs tell us that this is an adult male, maybe four years old. Only the males have spurs.

Only males have spurs on their feet.

The spurs deliver a wallop of venom. In fact, the platypus is the only truly venomous mammal. This animal doesn't use his spurs so much for defense as for combat during the breeding season, when males compete for access to females. The venom is strong enough to cause intense pain in human beings and can kill smaller animals like cats.

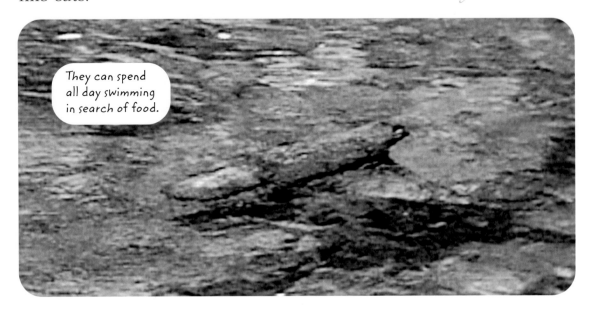

They can spend all day swimming in search of food.

The platypus spends most of its time diving and swimming, looking for food. Its scientific name is *Ornithorhynchus*, which means bird nose or beak faced, referring to the ducklike bill. If you look at the bill, you can see that it's covered with hundreds and hundreds of pores. And what are those pores for? They send out little electric impulses that sense food and other living animals in the water. It's almost like radar. The platypus swims with its eyes, ears,

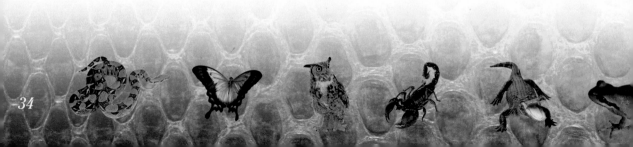

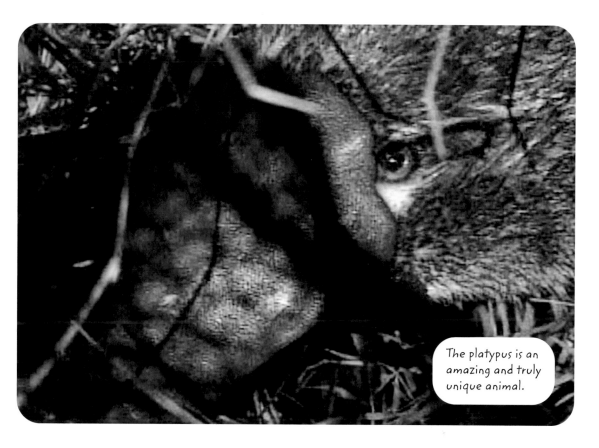

The platypus is an amazing and truly unique animal.

and nostrils closed. But the electric impulses bounce off everything around it. When the animal detects a little crustacean or other invertebrate, he gobbles it down.

Like the echidna, the platypus is a monotreme—an egg-laying mammal. A wonderful animal. I'm glad we got to see one. But he wasn't so happy to see us, and he wiggled free and swam off. He's probably headed for his burrow, somewhere along the stream bank.

The sun's finally out and maybe some sun-loving creatures will be too.

Let's see if we can find some snakes.

The hills above Hobart are alive with animals, and there are no signs of human development anywhere. We're finally getting a little sun. I'm enjoying the heat, and I'm hoping that some snakes and lizards will be out enjoying it too.

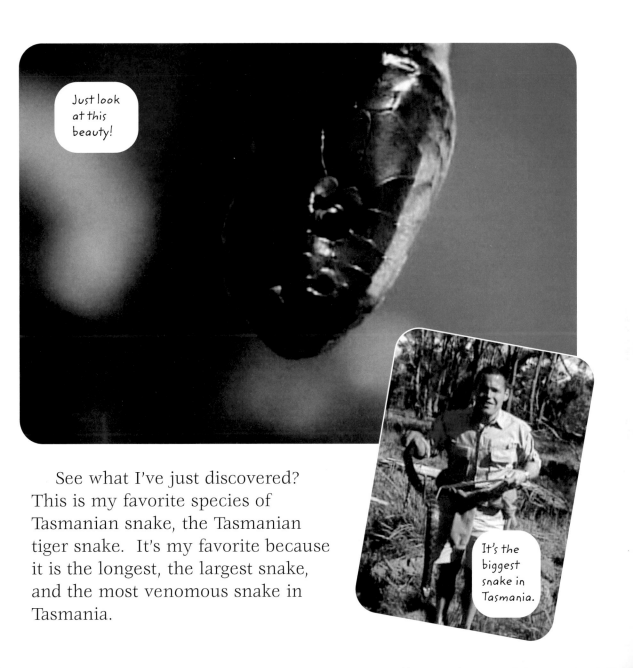

Just look at this beauty!

See what I've just discovered? This is my favorite species of Tasmanian snake, the Tasmanian tiger snake. It's my favorite because it is the longest, the largest snake, and the most venomous snake in Tasmania.

It's the biggest snake in Tasmania.

Two other snake species are found here as well. They are the white-lipped snake and the lowland copperhead, which we encountered earlier. All three belong to the same snake family. They are elapid snakes, and like all elapids they have a very potent type of venom called a neurotoxin. And this creature has the most potent venom of all here in Tasmania. In fact, the tiger snake is the fourth most venomous snake in the world. But fortunately, it's not particularly cantankerous. We caught this snake basking in the sun. Even though he's energized now, I don't have to pin him. I can just sort of work him on the stick.

Check this out. He's as thick as my wrist!

He's a heavy-bodied snake. As the largest snake in Tasmania, tiger snakes can grow to six feet in length and weigh a good six pounds. And as you can see, this one's almost as thick as my wrist. He's a very large and very beautiful snake.

Look at the colors—you can see why they call it a tiger snake, with those bands of yellow and black. There are many different color phases of these Tasmanian tiger snakes. You can find some that are solid black, some with really bright yellow colors, and some in which half the body has black and yellow stripes and the other half is jet black.

Yellow and black bands give this snake its name...

Like the other Tasmanian snakes, the tiger snakes are ovoviviparous—their young are born live. They can have up to 126 babies in one litter. And as a result they've established themselves pretty much through all of Tasmania, especially along rivers and in swamps or other wetlands. They feed on all sorts of things—lizards, birds, and especially frogs.

the Tasmanian tiger snake.

So many times people move to the country to be close to nature. And then sometimes nature, in the form of a snake like this, gets a little too close to them, and they don't like it. But as long as you respect this creature and give it the space it needs, you will have no problems with a tiger snake. So, let's place this one right down were we found it and continue on.

What kinds of creatures will the full moon bring out?

A brushtail possum!

Here, southeast of Hobart, we have finally arrived at one of the favorite haunts of the devil. After sunset and under a full moon, that's when these tassie devils like to party.

We're in a habitat with a lot of wildlife. I just spotted a brushtail possum, a tree dweller that's fairly common in these parts. That's not the creature we're here to find, but now I can hear the sound of a Tasmanian devil. Actually, it's the sound of a lot of Tasmanian devils. We're very close.

We're about to meet Tasmania's largest carnivorous marsupial. Pound for pound, this may be the fiercest animal on the planet. Imagine a pint-sized T. Rex, and then you have some idea of what meeting a tassie devil is like.

These Tasmanian devils are having a feast.

There they are, and they've got a kill. Now, I have to be careful here, because these guys don't like guests for dinner. We are surrounded by Tasmanian devils. They are feasting, they are crunching, and they are devouring what looks like at one time was some sort of macropod. My guess is a Bennetts wallaby.

You'll have to excuse me as I keep turning my head away from you. I'm not trying to be rude. I'm just trying to keep a good watch out for my backside and make sure nothing's going to take a nibble out of my buttocks. One of them just came right up to me. I had shoo it off and tell it that I'm not on the menu.

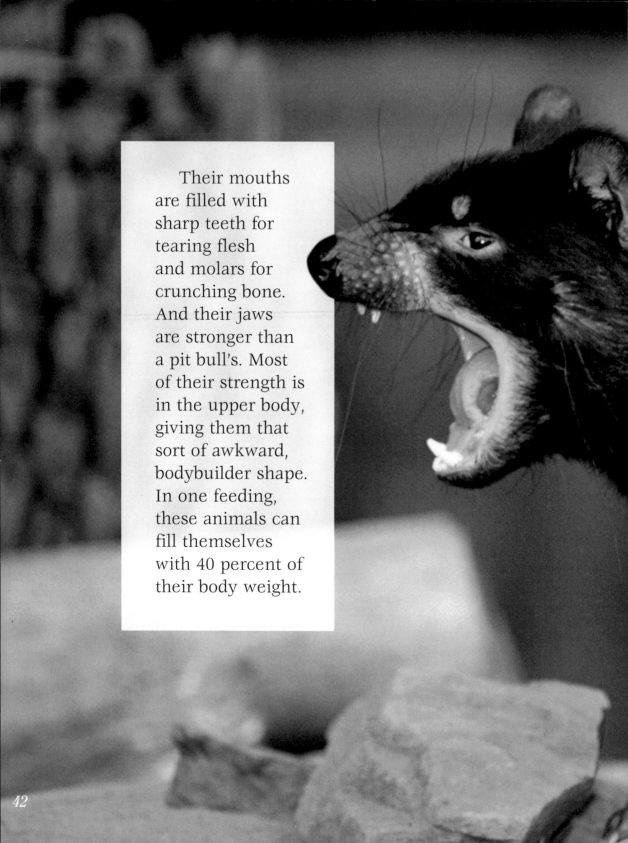

Their mouths are filled with sharp teeth for tearing flesh and molars for crunching bone. And their jaws are stronger than a pit bull's. Most of their strength is in the upper body, giving them that sort of awkward, bodybuilder shape. In one feeding, these animals can fill themselves with 40 percent of their body weight.

Tassie devils will share a large carcass.

With a small carcass, it's a different story.

Devils are by nature solitary animals. But in a situation like this, where there is a large carcass, these animals will come in and all feed on it at once. If this were a smaller carcass, there'd be a lot more battling going on. You'd hear a lot more

screeching. The devil's screech is its way of saying, "Stay away—this prey is mine." It's sort of a warning or a bluff. But that bluff is often crossed.

Now, there's plenty to go around. Let's be a little polite here, huh?

Well, friends, that wallaby is disappearing awfully fast. Before these creatures go from the appetizer to the entrée, I think we best

Then we'd hear a lot more screeching.

call it a night. But I hope you always cherish our journey here in Tasmania, one of my favorite places in the world to explore. It's a land filled with wonderful habitats and amazing animals, many found nowhere else but here.

Until we meet again, I'll be looking forward to our next great adventure.

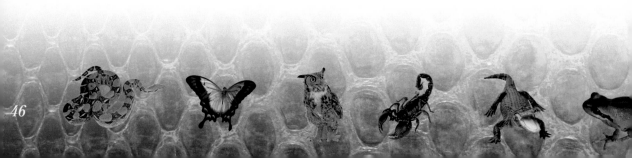

Glossary

carnivorous meat eating

crustacean a member of a group of animals that includes shrimp, crabs, pill bugs, and many small water dwellers

dingo Australian wild dog

diverse varied

environment the surroundings and conditions that affect living things and their ability to survive

evolved developed over many generations

extinct died out

feral escaped from domestication into the wild

habitat the place where a plant or animal naturally lives

incubate to keep eggs warm until hatching

invertebrate an animal without a backbone

macropods a group of marsupials that have powerful hind legs and move by jumping

mammals animals that have hair and (if female) produce milk to nourish their young

marsupials a group of mammals whose young are born at a very early stage of development; they continue their development attached to their mother, often in a pouch, feeding on her milk

monotreme a mammal that lays eggs

neurotoxin a poison that affects the nervous system

oviparous reproducing by laying eggs

ovoviviparous retaining eggs in the body and giving birth to live young

venomous poisonous

Index